India

A. Kamala Dalal

Ramesh C. Dhussa and Pradyumna P. Karan, Consultants

NATIONAL GEOGRAPHIC

WASHINGTON, D.C.

Contents

Foreword

For centuries, India has been imagined as a land of snake charmers, fabulous rulers called maharajas, and masses of poor people. Through a growing understanding of this diverse land and the massive developments taking place in India, this view has markedly changed. This enchanting land has a rich history and has experienced much change over the many years of its existence.

India is surrounded in the north by the world's loftiest mountain range, the Himalaya. In the southeast and southwest, it is bordered by the Arabian Sea and Bay of Bengal. These formidable natural barriers sheltered India from the outside world for a great part of its history. Around 2500 B.C., India gave birth to the Indus Valley Civilization. This is thought to be the world's first urban civilization. The first and second millennia B.C. saw the emergence of many other fascinating aspects of Indian civilization, such as the origin and evolution of the Hindu religion, the development of a social system based on strict ranks called castes, and great achievements in the areas of arts, sciences, mathematics, medicine, literature, and ethics.

In recent years India has made notable progress on its way to becoming a major political and economic power in the world. Developments in the fields of science, engineering, and the information technology industry have aided this advancement. Besides this, India's economy reflects development in transportation and other consumer goods industries, including automobile and railroad technologies. Present-day India can be described as a land with unity in diversity, with people from all walks of life, religions, and races.

This book appropriately highlights the spirit of the land called India. While on the one hand it will introduce you to the rich heritage of ancient India, it will also show you the changing landscapes that reflect the economic development of this fascinating country.

▲ Workers use high-power microscopes to check the quality of diamonds for export.

Ramesh C. Dhussa, Ph.D.
Drake University,
Des Moines, Iowa

From Monsoon to Drought

N JULY 2005, A NEW WORLD RECORD was set. In one 24-hour period, 37 inches (94 cm) of rain fell on the city of Mumbai (Bombay), on the west coast of India. Many people died and thousands of slum shacks were washed away in the torrential downpour. Indians are used to heavy rains during the annual monsoon, but no one could remember weather like that. Three years earlier, not far from Mumbai in the desert state of Rajasthan, the monsoon failed to arrive for the fourth year in a row, and the already dry land was baked to a hard crust. Wells ran dry and desperate people began moving to the cities. India's climate is dominated by the monsoons—strong winds that change direction with the seasons. They bring heavy rain from June to September.

◀ A tailor saves his sewing machine as monsoon rains flood the city of Porbandar on India's west coast.

WHAT'S THE WEATHER LIKE?

The villagers who live in the foothills of the mighty Himalaya see snow year-round and are used to temperatures that do not rise above 75° F (24° C). In the far south, people have never seen snow and are used to sun and constant heat year-round. India's varied terrain includes deserts, mountains, jungles, and beaches, so the weather varies accordingly. In general, winters are hot and dry, while the monsoon winds bring summer rain. The map opposite shows the physical features of India. Labels on this map and on similar maps throughout this book identify most of the places pictured in each chapter.

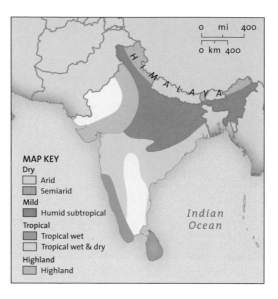

MAP KEY
Dry
☐ Arid
☐ Semiarid
Mild
■ Humid subtropical
Tropical
■ Tropical wet
☐ Tropical wet & dry
Highland
☐ Highland

Indian Ocean

Fast Facts

OFFICIAL NAME: Republic of India, Bharat
FORM OF GOVERNMENT: Federal republic
CAPITAL: New Delhi
POPULATION: 1,095,351,995
OFFICIAL LANGUAGES: Hindi (national language), English, and 21 other languages
MONETARY UNIT: Rupee
AREA: 1,269,345 square miles (3,287,590 square kilometers)
BORDERING NATIONS: Bangladesh, Bhutan, China, Myanmar, Nepal, and Pakistan
HIGHEST POINT: Kangchenjunga Mountain, 28,208 feet (8,598 m)
LOWEST POINT: sea level, 0 feet (0 m)
MAJOR MOUNTAIN RANGE: Himalaya
MAJOR RIVERS: Ganges, Yamuna, Indus, Brahmaputra

Average Temperature & Rainfall

Average High/Low Temperatures; Yearly Rainfall

DELHI (NORTH)
106° F (41° C) / 70° F (21° C); 28 in (71 cm)
MUMBAI (WEST COAST)
91° F (33° C) / 84° F (29° C); 102 in (260 cm)
CHENNAI (SOUTHEAST COAST)
100° F (38° C) / 82° F (28° C); 48 in (121 cm)
KOLKATA (EAST)
97° F (36° C) / 79° F (26° C); 62 in (157 cm)
DARJILING (FOOTHILLS)
68° F (20° C) / 48° F (9° C); 109 in (276 cm)
JAISALMER (DESERT)
108° F (42° C) / 75° F (24° C); 8 in (21 cm)

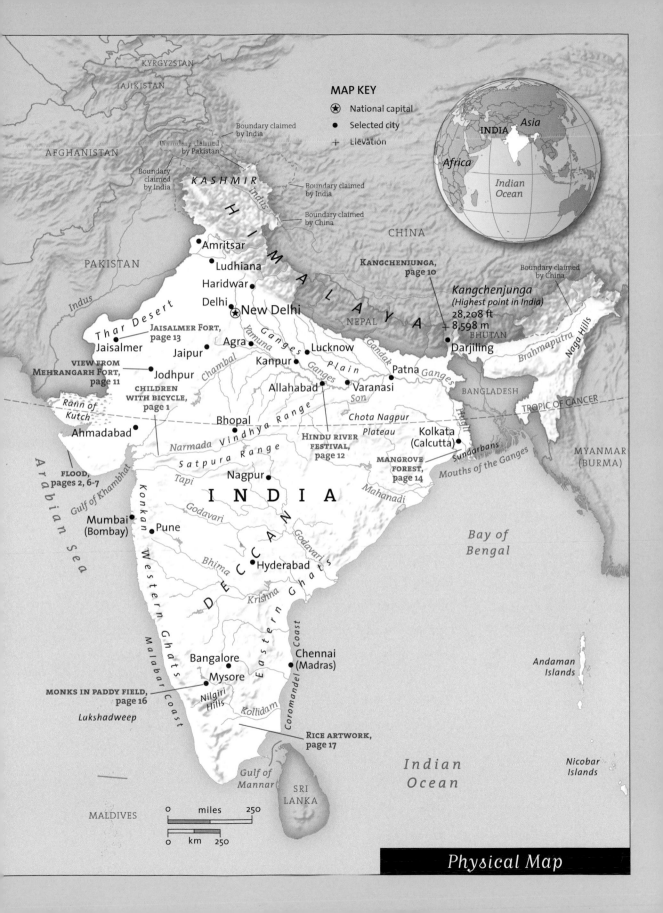

AFGHANISTAN

Boundary claimed
by India

Boundary claimed
by Pakistan

Boundary
claimed
by India

KASHMIR

Indus

Boundary claimed
by India

Boundary claimed
by China

CHINA

PAKISTAN

Indus

Amritsar

Ludhiana

Haridwar

Delhi

New Delhi

**KANGCHENJUNGA,
page 10**

Boundary claimed
by China

Kangchenjunga
(Highest point in India)
28,208 ft
+ 8,598 m

BHUTAN

Brahmaputra

Naga Hills

NEPAL

Thar Desert

**JAISALMER FORT,
page 13**

Jaisalmer

Jaipur

Agra

Yamuna

Kanpur

Lucknow

Ganges

Gandak

Darjiling

Plain

Patna

Ganges

**VIEW FROM
MEHRANGARH FORT,
page 11**

Jodhpur

Chambal

Ganges

Allahabad

Varanasi

BANGLADESH

**CHILDREN
WITH BICYCLE,
page 1**

Son

*Rann of
Kutch*

Bhopal

Narmada *Vindhya Range*

Chota Nagpur

Plateau

Kolkata
(Calcutta)

Sundarbans

TROPIC OF CANCER

MYANMAR
(BURMA)

Ahmadabad

Satpura Range

**HINDU RIVER
FESTIVAL,
page 12**

**MANGROVE
FOREST,
page 14**

Mouths of the Ganges

**FLOOD,
pages 2, 6-7**

Tapi

Nagpur

Mahanadi

A r a b i a n   S e a

Gulf of Khambhat

Godavari

INDIA

Konkan

Mumbai
(Bombay)

Pune

Bhima

Hyderabad

Godavari

*Bay of
Bengal*

D E C C A N

Krishna

Western Ghats

Eastern Ghats

*Andaman
Islands*

Malabar Coast

Bangalore

Chennai
(Madras)

**MONKS IN PADDY FIELD,
page 16**

Mysore

*Nilgiri
Hills*

Kollidam

Coromandel Coast

Lukshadweep

**RICE ARTWORK,
page 17**

*Gulf of
Mannar*

SRI
LANKA

*Indian
Ocean*

*Nicobar
Islands*

MALDIVES

0   miles   250

0   km   250

INDIA   *Asia*

Africa

*Indian
Ocean*

Physical Map

▲ The snow on Kangchenjunga Mountain glows in the sunset light. Its name means "the five treasures of snow," which refers to the mountain's five peaks. According to legend, the treasures represent the five storehouses of God: gold, silver, jewels, grain, and holy books.

The Top of the World

In the far north of India, forming a natural barrier with China, are the world's highest mountains, the snow-capped Himalaya. Buddhist pilgrims, traveling in ancient times, gave the range its name—*hima* is Sanskrit for "snow," and *alaya* means "abode," or home. The mountains appear in the Hindu religious epics (long poems about heroes and gods). The stepped shape of Hindu temples is intended to be a replica of the mighty mountains, where, Hindus believe, the gods live. Indians worship the Himalaya because they sustain life. Their snow melts into 19 major rivers, including the Indus, Ganges (Ganga), and

Brahmaputra, that flow across the plains of India.

The Himalaya are three parallel chains of mountains with deep valleys between them. The range stretches in a general direction of east to west over a distance of 1,553 miles (2,484 km). From north to south the range varies between 93 and 250 miles (148 and 400 km) in width.

THE EIGHT-THOUSANDERS

Ten of the highest peaks in the Himalaya are over 8,000 meters (26,000 ft) high. Only one is in India.

EVEREST	Nepal/China	8,848 meters (29,028 ft)
K2	Pakistan/China	8,611 meters (28,251 ft)
KANGCHENJUNGA	India/Nepal	8,598 meters (28,208 ft)
LHOTSE	Nepal/China	8,516 meters (27,940 ft)
MAKALU	Nepal/China	8,485 meters (27,838 ft)
CHO OYU	Nepal/China	8,188 meters (26,864 ft)
DHAULAGIRI	Nepal	8,167 meters (26,795 ft)
MANASLU	Nepal	8,163 meters (26,781 ft)
NANGA PARBUT	Pakistan	8,125 meters (26,657 ft)
ANNAPURNA I	Nepal	8,091 meters (26,545 ft)

The Ganges Plain

The Earth's surface is made up of huge plates that move in different directions and at different speeds. For millions of years, as the Indo-Australian and Eurasian plates collided, rocks were forced upward to form the Himalaya. As rivers cut through the rising rock, they carried vast amounts of soil down to the Ganges Plain below the mountains. In some places this layer of debris is over 25,000 feet (7,620 m) deep.

▼ The Mehrangarh Fort overlooks the blue houses of Jodhpur. The color is believed to help keep the houses cool and repel mosquitoes.

THE HOLY RIVER

The Ganges (Ganga) is more than a river for Indians. It is the source of life and death. The river is worshiped as the Hindu goddess Ganga, one of the two daughters of Meru (the Himalaya). At Haridwar, where the river emerges from its last rapids as it descends the mountains, the water is thought to be so holy that it can wash away even the worst sins. Haridwar is one of four holy sites where the Hindu god Vishnu is believed to have spilled a drop of nectar.

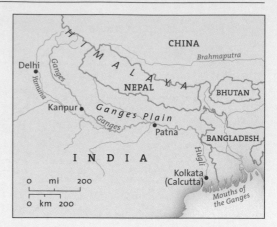

Every Hindu wants to visit the Ganges at some point in his or her life. Allahabad is where, according to Hindu mythology, the Ganges and Yamuna rivers meet Saraswati, the invisible River of Enlightenment. Every 12 years a religious fair, the Kumbh Mela, is held at Prayag Allahabad. In 2001 some 17 million people attended, making the event the largest human gathering ever.

At Varanasi (also called Banares), the river is lined with steps, or ghats, where worshipers come to wash themselves, drink the water, or make offerings. If possible Hindus want to die at Varanasi, and then be burned on one of the funeral ghats, which are kept piled high with wood. To die here is to be released from the cycle of life—repeated birth and death, or reincarnation. Many Hindus request that their ashes be sprinkled into the river.

▼ Crowds bathe in the Ganges River during the Kumbh Mela fair.

The process continues today: The Ganges River carries about a million tons of silt to the plain every year.

The silt makes the land very fertile, and as a result the plain is one of the world's most intensively farmed areas. Crops include rice, wheat, corn, sugarcane, and cotton. The fertile plain supports tens of thousands of villages, as well as some of India's largest cities.

The Peninsula

Most of India forms a peninsula, which looks like an upside-down triangle. In the west is the great Thar Desert. Despite a lack of water, the desert is home to some of India's most beautiful cities, including the "pink city" of Jaipur and the "blue city" of Jodhpur, both named for the color of their buildings.

▲ A caravan of camels crosses in front of the ruined fort at Jaisalmer. The city lies in the heart of the Thar Desert at a strategic stopping point on an ancient trade route used by Indian and Asian merchants. The route linked India to Central Asia and beyond. Today the camels are ridden by tourists who want to experience travel in the desert.

A TANGLED TALE

On the eastern edge of the Ganges Plain on the coast of the Bay of Bengal is a magical place where tigers swim in the same rivers as dolphins and sea turtles, while saltwater crocodiles lurk beneath the surface. Among the trees are six-foot (2 m) water monitor lizards, brilliant blue kingfishers, pythons, rhesus monkeys, wild pigs, and spotted deer. This is the Sandarbans, the world's biggest mangrove forest, which India shares with neighboring Bangladesh.

Mangrove trees are specially adapted to grow in salt water around the coastline. The tree's unusual, twisted root system helps it cope with strong currents and tides, as well as filtering out salt from the seawater drawn into the tree. The roots provide shelter for prawns, crabs, and shrimp.

The mangrove forest is also home to the world's largest single population of tigers. The majestic Royal Bengal tiger swims from island to island, covering as much as 25 miles (40 km) a day. Local villagers wear masks with painted faces on the back of their heads to scare away the tigers, which sometimes creep up on them as they chop wood or collect honey. Tigers are not the only danger. As women and children drag their nets along the shores to collect prawns to sell, they have to be on the alert for crocodiles and sharks.

This unique landscape is constantly under threat as sea levels rise and humans clear trees for firewood, hunt illegally, and create drainage ditches. Only 15 percent of the region is protected.

◀ The immense mangrove swamp of the Sundarbans seen from space

To the south of the Ganges Plain is the Deccan Plateau, which in the south is bordered on either side by hills, the Eastern and Western Ghats. The mountains are named for the steps that line the banks of the Ganges because they run parallel to the coast. They eventually meet in the far south of India as the

fertile Nilgiri Hills, which are covered with spice forests, tea plantations, and coffee bushes.

The Deccan Plateau is about 2,000 feet (600 m) high. It receives less rainfall than the plains below, and in the dry season its rivers dry up. When the monsoon rains arrive, fast-moving torrents of water create spectacular waterfalls that tumble over the edges of the plateau. Large fortresses, built by some of India's former rulers, dominate the plateau ridges.

Coasts and Beaches

The strip of coastal plain between the Arabian Sea and the northern part of the Western Ghats is called the Konkan. Only about one-third of the land is suitable for farming, and most people live in the river valleys and in industrial areas around cities such as Mumbai.

▲ Fishers and villagers join forces to pull in the fishing nets on India's west coast.

Some of the world's most beautiful beaches lie between Goa and Kerala in the far south. Inland from the Keralan beaches are the backwaters, a series of narrow, natural canals that crisscross the landscape. The canals are lined with houses, coconut palms, and rubber trees. In the past, villagers used 80-foot (24 m) boats to transport rice, coconuts, and other goods to coastal ports. The *kettuvallom*, or "boat with knots," was held together with coir rope made from the fibrous husks of coconuts. Not a single nail was used. Part of the boat was covered with bamboo and coir

▼ Buddhist monks tend their rice plants near the city of Mysore. Rice seedlings are planted by hand in flooded fields called paddies. To harvest the rice, the water is drained from the field.

matting to serve as living quarters for the crew. Today many kettuvallom have been converted to houseboats so that tourists can explore the canals in comfort.

Many of India's major rivers reach the sea on the east coast, which means that the coastal plain has been formed by deep layers of sediment. The deltas, or river mouths, are a maze of shifting channels, and ocean tides can reach far inland. Even a small rise in sea level would submerge the large city of Kolkata (Calcutta), which is about 95 miles (153 km) inland.

The southern state of Tamil Nadu is one of India's most fertile regions and is often called the "rice bowl of India." The women of Tamil Nadu use finely ground rice flour and coloring to make elaborate, sacred drawings called *kolam* on moistened ground in front of their houses. Young girls learn the patterns from their mothers, grandmothers, or aunts.

▲ Young women in Tamil Nadu create colorful *kolam* artworks outside their house during Pongal, the Hindu harvest festival.

Animals
and
Gods

LYING IN THE MIDDLE of a busy street, amid the traffic and crowds, is a group of cows. Buses, taxis, motorbikes, and automobiles swerve to avoid hitting them. For thousands of years, since Hinduism first evolved as a religion, respect for animal life has been an important part of Indians' beliefs. Cows, in particular, are sacred to Hindus and cannot be harmed. But as cities have grown more crowded, the thousands of cows that share the streets with residents pose an increasing problem. They rip open garbage bags in search of food. And, of course, they add to the traffic chaos. Some cities have hired men to catch cows and release them outside the city or place them in special reserves where the animals can be cared for.

◀ Cows are useful for pulling plows or carts and providing milk or manure that can be dried and used as a fuel for fires—but they cause chaos in city streets.

LIONS AND TIGERS

Animals are part of everyday and religious life in India, even in the city. Certain animals are revered for their divine qualities. Hindus respect cows, Buddhists regard the cobra as sacred, and the Toda people of South India believe that buffalo are equal to humans.

India's varied vegetation zones—or what grows where—are shown on the map opposite. They support a wealth of wildlife: 65,000 species of animal and 13,000 types of flowering plant. India is the only country in the world with both lions and tigers.

India is a bird watcher's paradise. The Sarus crane stands as tall as a man at 6 feet (2 m) and the Himalayan bearded vulture has a wingspan of 8 feet (2.5 m). Tickell's flowerpecker, in contrast, is the size of a thumb. The hill myna is famous for its ability as a mimic; in captivity the birds soon learn to speak.

▶ **The lion-tailed macaque is a rare species. It lives only in India's Western Ghats.**

Species at Risk

India is at a critical point. Its population has grown to over one billion people, and its economy is booming. As a result there is growing concern about the survival of the country's natural areas. People cut down trees for firewood, to make furniture, and to clear land for farming. Other habitats, such as wetlands, are also being destroyed or damaged. Animals are being hunted illegally for food or trade.

Species at risk include:
> Asian elephant
> Asiatic black bear
> Asiatic lion
> Bengal fox
> Ganges river dolphin
> Gaur (Indian bison)
> Golden langur (monkey)
> Great Indian bustard (bird)
> Great one-horned rhinoceros
> Himalayan musk deer
> Indian python
> Indian star tortoise
> Indian wolf
> Kashmir stag
> King cobra
> Lion-tailed macaque
> Nilgiri tahr (goat)
> Olive ridley turtle
> Sarus crane
> Sloth bear
> Snow leopard
> Swamp deer
> Tiger
> White-winged duck

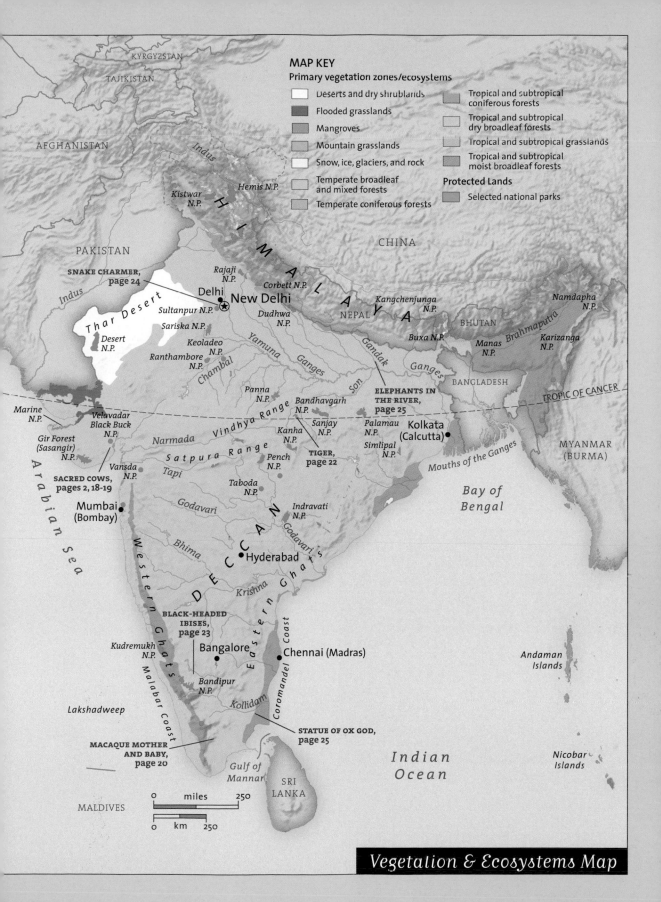

MAP KEY

Primary vegetation zones/ecosystems

Deserts and dry shrublands
Flooded grasslands
Mangroves
Mountain grasslands
Snow, ice, glaciers, and rock
Temperate broadleaf and mixed forests
Temperate coniferous forests
Tropical and subtropical coniferous forests
Tropical and subtropical dry broadleaf forests
Tropical and subtropical grasslands
Tropical and subtropical moist broadleaf forests

Protected Lands

Selected national parks

KYRGYZSTAN

TAJIKISTAN

AFGHANISTAN

PAKISTAN

Indus

CHINA

NEPAL

BHUTAN

Brahmaputra

BANGLADESH

MYANMAR (BURMA)

H I M A L A Y A

Kistwar N.P.

Hemis N.P.

Rajaji N.P.

Corbett N.P.

Kangchenjunga N.P.

Namdapha N.P.

SNAKE CHARMER, page 24

Delhi ⊛ New Delhi

Indus

Thar Desert

Sultanpur N.P.

Dudhwa N.P.

Buxa N.P.

Manas N.P.

Karizanga N.P.

Desert N.P.

Sariska N.P.

Keoladeo N.P.

Ranthambore N.P.

Chambal

Yamuna

Ganges

Gandak

Son

Ganges

TROPIC OF CANCER

Marine N.P.

Panna N.P.

Bandhavgarh N.P.

ELEPHANTS IN THE RIVER, page 25

Gir Forest (Sasangir) N.P.

Velavadar Black Buck N.P.

Narmada

Vindhya Range

Sanjay N.P.

Kanha N.P.

Palamau N.P.

Simlipal N.P.

Kolkata (Calcutta)

SACRED COWS, pages 2, 18-19

Vansda N.P.

Satpura Range

Tapi

Pench N.P.

TIGER, page 22

Mouths of the Ganges

Bay of Bengal

Taboda N.P.

Godavari

Indravati N.P.

Mumbai (Bombay)

A r a b i a n   S e a

D E C C A N

Bhima

Hyderabad

Godavari

Krishna

BLACK-HEADED IBISES, page 23

Western Ghats

Eastern Ghats

Kudremukh N.P.

Bangalore

Chennai (Madras)

Andaman Islands

Coromandel Coast

Bandipur N.P.

Malabar Coast

Kollidam

STATUE OF OX GOD, page 25

Lakshadweep

MACAQUE MOTHER AND BABY, page 20

Gulf of Mannar

SRI LANKA

I n d i a n   O c e a n

Nicobar Islands

MALDIVES

0   miles   250

0   km   250

Vegetation & Ecosystems Map

High in the Himalaya

The Himalaya provide a home for some of India's rarest animals and plants. The most elusive of Indian animals is the snow leopard. Its wailing calls are often mistaken for those of the yeti—a mythical mountain monster. The leopard preys on muntjac. Muntjac are also called barking deer because they make a deep barking noise when alarmed. Bears and black buck live lower down

PROJECT TIGER

Hundreds of years ago the tiger roamed forests and jungles throughout India. At the beginning of the 19th century there were 40,000 tigers in India. By 1972 there were fewer than 2,000 left. People realized that they had to do something to save the tiger, and Project Tiger was launched. It led to a ban on tiger hunting and the establishment of 27 tiger reserves. By the 1990s the number of tigers had grown to around 3,500.

But, once again, the tiger is fighting for survival. Illegal hunting has increased, driven by a demand for tiger bones, which are highly prized in other parts of the world for traditional medicine, and tiger skins.

In remote villages the tiger can be a serious threat. Every year people are attacked and killed, which leads to revenge killing of the tigers. This happens more often now because a growing human population has reduced the tiger's habitat and brought tigers and villagers closer together. Despite all these problems, 18 of India's states still have tiger populations and conservationists around the world are working hard to save them.

◀ Tiger cubs remain with their mother for about two years after their birth.

in the flower-filled rhododendron forests. In the extreme northeast of the mountain range, the tiger and the one-horned rhinoceros can be found.

Plants cannot grow above 14,400 feet (4,400 m). Below that, they have adapted to the extreme cold and strong winds by growing low to the ground.

▲ Black-headed ibises live in marshy areas and along the coast, where they feed on frogs, fish, and insects.

Fertile Plain to Desert

In the far west of India is the vast Thar Desert, which stretches from India to Pakistan. It is the natural habitat of the camel, which is a popular form of transportation for people in the isolated desert villages. In contrast, the

◄ Ancient Hindu holy men were struck by the eternal cycle of life—a caterpillar becomes a butterfly and then lays eggs that hatch into new caterpillars. Human souls, they believed, also go through this cycle by being reincarnated, or born again.

WHERE THE COBRA IS KING

▲ Snake charmers generally remove their snakes' fangs before handling or "charming" them.

The world's longest poisonous snake, the king cobra, is equally revered and feared across India. Images of the Hindu god Shiva show him with a king cobra draped around his neck. The king cobra has a special festival—Nagapanchami—held every summer to honor it.

In 2006 a village woman in Orissa even married a king cobra because she believed it had helped her get better when she fell sick. Two thousand people attended the wedding.

Snake charmers are a common sight in India playing music to a cobra in a basket. The cobra remains in strike pose with its hood expanded, hypnotized by the charmer's movements rather than by the music, since snakes are deaf.

In the wild, king cobras live in the cool undergrowth of rain forests. However, deforestation, due to growing populations and agriculture, is reducing the forests, and the king cobra is endangered.

fertile Ganges Plain supports a wide variety of animal life, including many different kinds of bird. In the far east are the Sundarbans, a network of tidal rivers and flat, marshy islands covered with mangrove forest, which is one of the last preserves of the Bengal tiger.

The Asiatic lion once lived all across Asia, but now only 350 of them live wild in the Gir Forest in western India. These lions have a shorter mane than their African relatives. India was also once home to many wild elephants. There are several differences between Indian and African elephants. The Indian elephant is smaller in size with smaller ears, and the females do not have tusks. The country still has many elephants, but most of them are tame and live with people. They are used for transportation and as heavy lifters on construction sites. Each working elephant has a keeper,

called a *mahout*, to look after it. A young boy will grow up with his elephant, and they remain together until one of them dies. A mahout spends time washing, feeding, and caring for his elephant. Man and animal develop a bond that allows the mahout to control the elephant with verbal commands and touch. But the elephant is still unpredictable, and the mahout has to be alert, especially during the mating season when male elephants become very aggressive.

▲ At sunrise mahouts take their elephants to the Gandak River to scrub them clean, decorate them, and take them to the Sonepur Mela, Asia's largest cattle fair. Horses and elephants are sold at the fair, which lasts for two weeks.

MOTHER COW

According to ancient Indian scriptures, the cow is a gift of the gods to humans. The cow represents the mother goddess, who looks after humans just as the cow looks after her calf. Her sacred gifts are milk, curds (yogurt), butter, urine (used in medicine), and manure (used as fuel for fires). Every part of the cow's body has a religious significance. Its horns symbolize the gods, its face the sun and moon, its shoulders the god of fire (Agni), and its legs the Himalaya. Killing cows is illegal in most Indian states.

▲ A temple priest pours milk colored with turmeric over a statue of Nandi, the ox ridden by the Hindu god Shiva.

A Blend of many Cultures

THE TAJ MAHAL HAS BEEN CALLED a love letter in stone. Emperor Shah Jehan was heartbroken when his beloved wife, Mumtaz Mahal, died in childbirth. He decided to build the world's most beautiful tomb in her memory. It would be made entirely of white marble, decorated with semiprecious stones. The tomb would be set in a formal garden with avenues, fountains, and a pool that reflected the Taj. Building started in 1631. One thousand elephants carried the white marble from Rajasthan to Agra, where 20,000 workers labored for more than 20 years. At the very center of the building is Mumtaz Mahal's white marble casket. According to legend, Shah Jehan planned a black marble tomb for himself, but it was never built. Instead, he was laid to rest next to his wife.

◄ As a symbol of undying love, the Taj Mahal has become a place of pilgrimage. It is visited by more than two million people every year.

THE INDUS PEOPLES

In the 1920s archaeologists explored the long-buried ruins of two huge cities, dating back to about 3000 B.C., in the valley of the Indus River. They named the cities Harappa and Mohenjo Daro. Although both sites are now in Pakistan, the Indus civilization is connected to later Indian cultures, such as the Dravidians.

The Indus peoples lived in brick houses up to three stories high, arranged along streets planned on a grid system. The houses had a piped water supply and bathrooms linked to sewers. No other ancient civilization had anything like it. The Indus peoples seem to have been peaceful and prosperous. They grew wheat and cotton and used metals to make tools. Their society was ruled by priests.

The Harappans could write—but no one has been able to read their writing. Nobody knows why the cities were abandoned in about 1700 B.C. It may have been because of flooding or invasion by a more warlike culture.

▲ **Archaeologists think that this figure from Mohenjo Daro was a priest king.**

Time line

This chart shows the approximate dates for some of the major peoples to dominate India throughout its long history. Some of the rulers were native to the region; others were invaders.

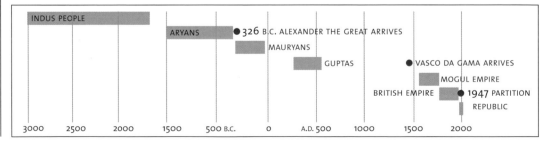

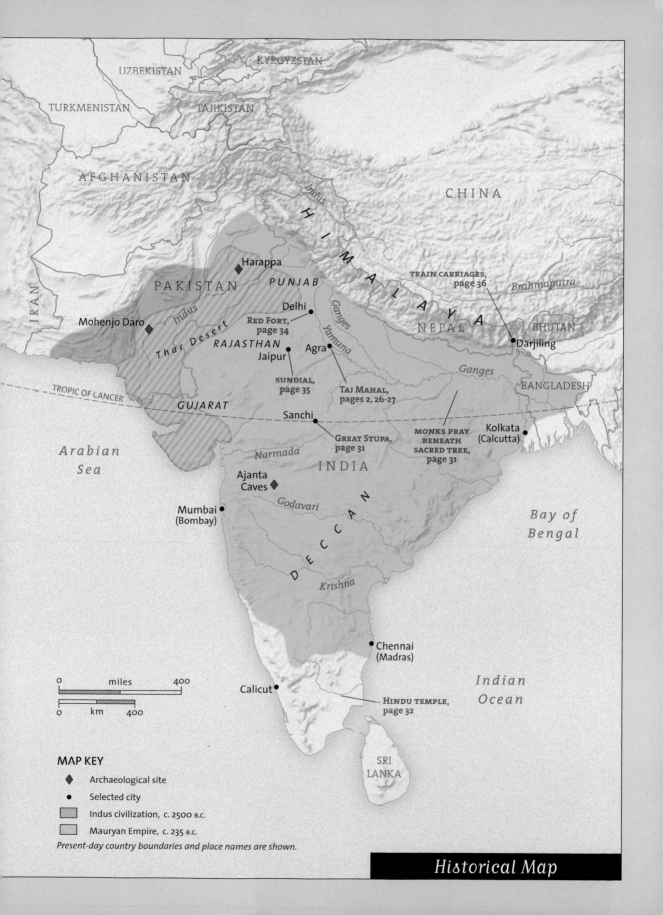

UZBEKISTAN

KYRGYZSTAN

TURKMENISTAN

TAJIKISTAN

AFGHANISTAN

CHINA

Indus

H I M A L A Y A

Harappa

TRAIN CARRIAGES,
page 36

Brahmaputra

PAKISTAN

PUNJAB

IRAN

Delhi

RED FORT,
page 34

Ganges

NEPAL

BHUTAN

Mohenjo Daro

Indus

Yamuna

Darjiling

Thar Desert

RAJASTHAN

Agra

Jaipur

SUNDIAL,
page 35

TAJ MAHAL,
pages 2, 26-27

Ganges

BANGLADESH

TROPIC OF LANCER

GUJARAT

Sanchi

GREAT STUPA,
page 31

MONKS PRAY
BENEATH
SACRED TREE,
page 31

Kolkata
(Calcutta)

Arabian
Sea

Narmada

I N D I A

Ajanta
Caves

Godavari

D
E
C
C
A
N

Bay of
Bengal

Mumbai
(Bombay)

Krishna

Chennai
(Madras)

Indian
Ocean

Calicut

HINDU TEMPLE,
page 32

0   miles   400

0   km   400

SRI
LANKA

MAP KEY

◆   Archaeological site

•   Selected city

      Indus civilization, c. 2500 B.C.

      Mauryan Empire, c. 235 B.C.

Present-day country boundaries and place names are shown.

Historical Map

The Aryans

The Aryan people were farmers from Central Asia who arrived in India around 1500 B.C. when the Harappan civilization was all but over. The Aryans spoke Sanskrit, one of the world's oldest known languages and the origin of most of the languages spoken in India today. They had advanced weapons, including war chariots, and were able to push India's earlier inhabitants, the Dravidians, south to the region where they still live.

Over the centuries, Aryan society developed into the system of social ranks, or castes, that still influences Indian society today. Caste is determined by birth and there is almost no way to change it. Members of a caste can marry only within the group. The highest castes are the priests, followed by landowners, soldiers, and then craftsmen. Untouchables have no caste and do the most menial jobs.

The Vedic Scriptures, which form the basis of the Hindu religion, were written sometime between 1500 and 1200 B.C. *Veda* means "knowledge." The Aryans worshiped many different gods, but they believed these gods were different aspects of one divine power. Hindus still believe this today.

▼ The Hindu god Garuda has the body of a man and the wings of an eagle. Followers believe that worship of Garuda will remove poisons from the body.

Greeks and Buddhists

In the fourth century B.C., the Greek general Alexander the Great led an army across Asia and arrived in India in 326 B.C. He took control of the Punjab, a fertile area now split between India and Pakistan. However, he was prevented from traveling further east because his troops had been away from home for so long that they refused to keep fighting. Alexander left India and died soon after.

A dynasty named the Mauryans took control of the Punjab and then most of India. They were a farming

▲ Buddhist monks pray beneath a pipal tree known as the Bodhi tree. Under it, Buddha is believed to have attained enlightenment.

STUNNING STUPAS

The founder of Buddhism, a prince named Siddhartha Gautama, was born in 563 B.C. He became a beggar and spent years wandering through India. Finally, he achieved enlightenment. From this moment, he was known as the Buddha, or "Enlightened One." Buddhists believe that enlightenment is a way to

▲ The Great Stupa is the largest of several stupas at Sanchi.

achieve nirvana, or release from suffering. It is possible to attain nirvana by rejecting worldly goods and behaving with kindness.

The stupa, a stone dome, is a distinctive Buddhist form of architecture. The shape is based on an upside-down begging bowl. Pilgrims walk around the main dome, which may contain relics from the Buddha or other holy men. Stupas were built across India in the third century B.C.

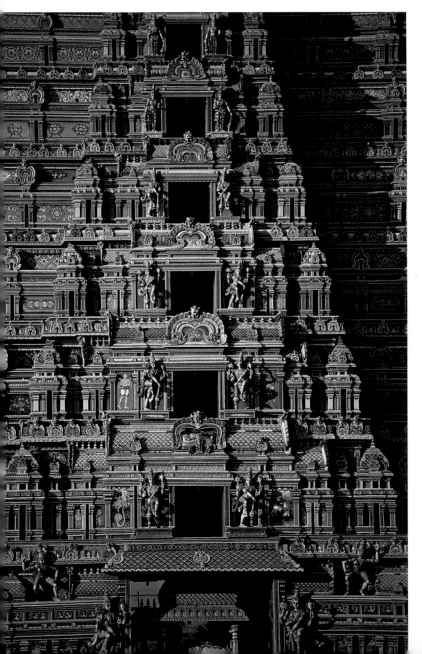

Sri Ranganathaswamy Temple in Tamil Nadu, in the far south of India, is the world's largest Hindu temple still in use, and has been in place for 2,000 years. This part of the temple complex is known as the Hall of 1,000 Pillars.

society. The Mauryans were the first native people to unify most of India, except the Tamils in the south—the descendents of the Dravidians. The Mauryan Empire's greatest ruler was Asoka, who ruled from 272 to 232 B.C. He turned against war and converted to the new religion of Buddhism. Asoka spent the rest of his reign encouraging the spread of nonviolence, vegetarianism, and pilgrimage.

Rise and Fall

India, especially the northern areas, then entered a period of upheaval as many more rulers and empires battled for control. It was not until the Gupta Empire in the fourth century A.D. that India had its next period of stability. For 200 years, arts, crafts, and sciences flourished. The Indian astronomer Aryabhatta worked out that the Earth revolved around the sun long before the Western world accepted the theory. Gupta power was shattered by Mongol invaders from Central Asia. For the next five centuries, the north once more relapsed into chaos, but in the far south, a separate Hindu culture continued to flourish.

Mogul Splendor

Beginning in the 11th century, a succession of Muslim invaders swept across India with varying amounts of success. In the 14th century, the Mongol leader Timur, or Tamerlane, attacked the plains of northern India. In the 16th century, Babur, a descendant of Tamerlane, founded the Mogul Empire, bringing two centuries of peace, prosperity, and magnificence to India.

A GOLDEN AGE

Mogul rulers oversaw a golden age of art, literature, and architecture between 1527 and 1707. They built mosques, gardens, and tombs, including the Taj Mahal at Agra. They also created a network of roads and established an efficient administration.

The most able Mogul ruler was Akbar, who became emperor at age 13. Even though he was a Muslim, he married a Hindu woman and employed Hindu advisors, which helped keep the empire stable. He loved literature and art, particularly miniatures. Courtiers read to him for several hours a day, and he held many discussions with famous scholars.

▲ Muslim artists are forbidden to make pictures of people or animals. Mogul artists concentrated on beautiful writing called calligraphy or on intricate patterns like these that decorate the Taj Mahal.

Aurangzeb, the great-grandson of Emperor Akbar, lacked his ancestor's diplomatic skills. He tried to make the whole country Islamic and started to tax his people heavily. Both moves were unpopular and led to rebellions. His unsuccessful military campaigns into the south damaged the economy. With his death in 1707, the Mogul Empire began to weaken. Successive rulers, such as the Marathas in the 18th century, followed, but fighting between different groups left India vulnerable to invasion by European powers.

The Europeans Arrive

The Portuguese were the first Europeans to arrive in India, when the explorer Vasco da Gama reached Kerala in 1498. Portugal set up a colony in the state

▼ The Red Fort is one of the most famous buildings in Delhi. It was built as a palace for the Mogul emperor Shah Jehan. Today it is one of the country's most popular tourist destinations.

of Goa on the west coast early in the 16th century and kept it until 1961.

Indian spices were highly prized in 16th-century Europe. There was no way of preserving meat, and spices helped disguise the taste when it began to rot. Spices became more valuable than gold. The British, French, Dutch, and Danish also set up trading companies in India. But Britain and France had wider ambitions; they wanted to take control of the country. After a number of battles between the two countries, the British gained effective control of most of India in 1757. (The French retained a few small coastal colonies until 1954.)

The British Empire

With victory, the British set about changing their role from traders to rulers. The British East India Company, set up to organize trade with India, grew more powerful and began to control other aspects of Indian life. Soon the British government was running the country in place of the East India Company.

▲ This huge sundial was built in the late 17th century by astronomers in the service of Sawai Jai Singh, the first maharaja of the kingdom of Amber (later called Jaipur). Jai Singh built five huge observatories to explore the night skies. At the time, nothing similar existed in the West.

THE TOY TRAIN THROUGH THE MOUNTAINS

Many British in India hated the hot summers. They escaped to the mountains, where the air was cooler. But the so-called hill stations were hard to get to. The tea grown there was also hard to get down to the lowlands. The British decided to build a railroad to the tea town of Darjiling. But they faced a huge challenge: the Himalaya.

Engineer Franklin Prestage worked out how to get a train up the mountains after his wife gave him a dancing lesson. She told him to go back to go forward. Every time the slope got too steep, Franklin brought the track back in a zigzag so it climbed again from a new point. No other railroad in the world works like this.

Alongside the tracks are the famous tea plantations. Tea grows at high elevations, and the tea of Darjiling is of a very high quality. Women still pluck the leaves of the plants by hand before they are dried and processed.

◀ The Darjiling train is scaled down to fit the narrow track. It is known as the "toy train."

▼ Darjiling was built by the British, who spent the summers in hill towns, or "stations," to escape the hot plains.

At the start of the 19th century, India was made up of states ruled by princes, or maharajas. The British embarked on a program to unite the country. They constructed roads and railroads, introduced British

forms of government, and made English the official language.

Independence

The first major uprising against the British was in 1856, but it was not until the 20th century that protest became organized. After World War I (1914–18), a man emerged who would lead the push for independence—Mahatma Gandhi.

When World War II (1939–45) ended, Britain could no longer afford to keep India. Muslims began to fight Hindus for control, and it became clear that India would have to be divided into separate Muslim and Hindu states.

On August 15, 1947, India became independent as a mainly Hindu country. The new Muslim country of Pakistan was granted independence a day earlier. Some 13 million Hindus and Muslims were forced to move between the new countries. Violence erupted and about one million people died. India and Pakistan went to war almost at once over Kashmir. The dispute over the state still goes on.

MAHATMA GANDHI

Mahatma means "Great Soul" and was the affectionate name given to Mohandas Gandhi by Indians. Gandhi is the most famous Indian in history, not just because he was the driving force behind India's move for independence but also because of the means he used to achieve peace.

Gandhi was born into a wealthy, devout Hindu family and trained in London, England, to be a lawyer. He gave up his successful practice in Mumbai to move to South Africa, where he campaigned for the rights of Indian workers who were being discriminated against because of their color.

Gandhi returned to India in 1914, famous for his nonviolent protests in South Africa. His travels across India shocked him as he saw how the Untouchables, who do India's worst jobs, were treated. He started to wear the loincloth, the dress of the Untouchables.

He became the leader of the Indian National Congress in 1920 and, using nonviolent protests, set about ridding India of the British. The British imprisoned Gandhi on many occasions, and he went on hunger strikes as another means of protest. A year after India gained independence, Gandhi was killed by a Hindu who objected to his tolerance toward other faiths.

▶ A statue of Gandhi in Kerala

Families
and
Festivals

N INDIA, IT'S EASY TO TELL if a Hindu woman has just gotten married. For weeks after the wedding, her hands and perhaps her feet are stained with a brown-red pattern. In some regions, the husband also has dyed hands. The dyeing, called *mehendi*, is said to bring good luck to a marriage. The day before the wedding, the bride's family and friends gather to draw the designs in a paste made from henna. The bride sits very still while the paste dries. She must be patient: it takes several hours to dry. Then the paste is washed off, leaving the pattern dyed on her skin. Mehendi is just one part of the wedding. Celebrations can last for days, with hundreds of guests. People often travel a long way to attend the lavish family celebrations.

◄ The patterns on a bride's hand often contain the initials of the couple being married. If the groom can find the initials, it is thought to be a lucky sign for the wedding.

A Rural Population

Nearly three-quarters of India's one billion people live in the countryside. Most live in some 600,000 villages where the way of life has changed little for centuries.

The city with the biggest population is Mumbai, the financial center of India, with more than 16 million people. The city has grown quickly. In the 1950s its population was only 3.5 million. Most of the people who come to Mumbai want to find a job that will bring them a better way of life. Many villagers live in poverty, and job opportunities are limited. Some move into cities temporarily when there is little work at home. They go back to their villages for the harvest.

COMMON INDIAN PHRASES

Hindi is India's national language. Here are some common Hindi words and phrases for you to try out:

Namaste (nuh-MUS-stay) Hello or goodbye
Aap kaiseh hein? (aap KAY-se hain) How are you?
Haan (han) Yes
Nahin (nah-hin) No
Mehar-bani seh (may-har ban-ee say) Please
Dhanyavaad (DUN-y e vaad) Thank you

▶ Crowds of pedestrians and cars share the road in a busy Indian city street.

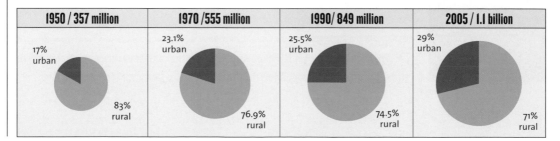

1950 / 357 million	1970 / 555 million	1990 / 849 million	2005 / 1.1 billion
17% urban / 83% rural	23.1% urban / 76.9% rural	25.5% urban / 74.5% rural	29% urban / 71% rural

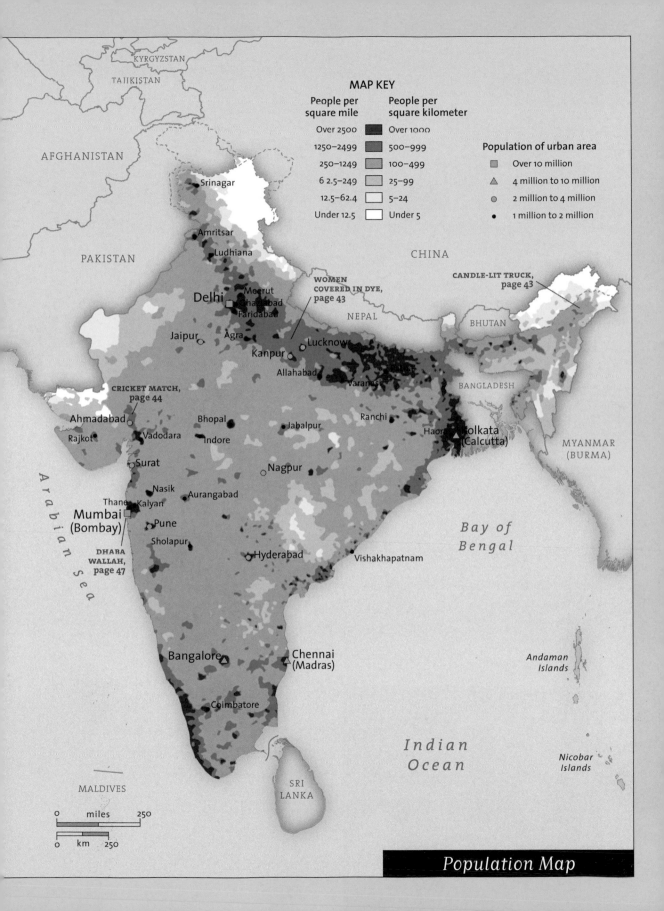

MAP KEY

People per square mile		People per square kilometer
Over 2500		Over 1000
1250–2499		500–999
250–1249		100–499
62.5–249		25–99
12.5–62.4		5–24
Under 12.5		Under 5

Population of urban area

- ■ Over 10 million
- ▲ 4 million to 10 million
- ● 2 million to 4 million
- • 1 million to 2 million

KYRGYZSTAN

TAJIKISTAN

AFGHANISTAN

PAKISTAN

CHINA

Srinagar

Amritsar

Ludhiana

Delhi

Meerut
Ghaziabad
Faridabad

WOMEN
COVERED IN DYE,
page 43

CANDLE-LIT TRUCK,
page 43

NEPAL

BHUTAN

Jaipur

Agra

Kanpur

Lucknow

Allahabad

Varanasi

BANGLADESH

CRICKET MATCH,
page 44

Bhopal

Jabalpur

Ranchi

Ahmadabad

Rajkot

Vadodara

Indore

Haora Kolkata
(Calcutta)

MYANMAR
(BURMA)

Surat

Nagpur

Nasik

Aurangabad

Thane Kalyan

Mumbai
(Bombay)

Pune

DHABA
WALLAH,
page 47

Sholapur

Hyderabad

Vishakhapatnam

Bay of
Bengal

Arabian
Sea

Andaman
Islands

Bangalore

Chennai
(Madras)

Coimbatore

Indian
Ocean

Nicobar
Islands

MALDIVES

SRI
LANKA

0 miles 250

0 km 250

Population Map

NATIONAL HOLIDAYS

India has only three national holidays, but if you visit for more than a few days, you will probably run into a celebration. There are so many different gods that religious festivals happen all the time. One of the most important Hindu occasions is Diwali, the festival of lights, which takes place in either October or November. Diwali gets its name from the candles and lamps in homes and streets, and the fireworks that light the night sky. Chalk designs called *rangolis* are painted on the ground to welcome the Hindu gods back to Earth. Indians love fireworks, so they start shooting them off days before the actual festival.

Christians celebrate Easter and Christmas, while Ramadan and Eid al-Fitr are the most important Islamic festivals. Each state also has its own holidays.

JANUARY 26	Republic Day
AUGUST 15	Independence Day
OCTOBER 2	Gandhi Jayanti (Mahatma Gandhi's birthday)

Getting Married

A wedding is a highlight for any Indian family. It is still common for two families to arrange a marriage between their children. Sunday newspapers in Indian cities have pages and pages of advertisements from families looking for a husband or wife for a daughter or son. The advertisements specify exactly what a family is looking for.

If families agree to a match, the future bride and groom meet. Often, the marriage goes ahead only if they agree to it. Many couples in arranged marriages fall in love after they are married. Today, a growing number of young people, especially in the larger cities, find their own partners by dating.

In a traditional home, a new wife moves in with her husband's family. She takes over the running of the home from her mother-in-law.

The Heart of Life

The family is at the heart of Indian life. Parents, children, aunts, uncles, and grandparents traditionally share

▼ Three generations of a family celebrate the 50th Indian Independence Day with a picnic.

HOLI HOLIDAY

If you ever visit India and someone you don't know throws colored powder over you, it means that you have arrived during the Hindu festival of Holi. The most colorful of India's festivals marks the start of spring. It is always celebrated on the day of the full moon in March.

The night before Holi, people light bonfires to say goodbye to the winter. They gather at temples to sing and dance to music. But the real fun starts on the day of Holi. It is traditional to throw *gulal*—bright powders and

▲ Women try to protect themselves against a shower of water mixed with dye.

water—at anybody and everybody! People often wear their oldest clothes because they know they cannot avoid being hit. For days afterward, stains remain on peoples' clothes.

the same house. More families now consist of just parents and their children, but they still have strong links with their other relatives. Everyone in the family gives one another economic and emotional support when it is needed. Old people are respected for their age and wisdom.

▼ A man decorates his truck with candles to celebrate Diwali.

"Polite Baseball"

Many parts of Indian life still show the influence of Britain, which governed the country for nearly two centuries. The

▲ Boys play a game of cricket in northern Gujarat. Their small village has no sports facilities, so they have made their own equipment.

British brought cricket to India in the 18th century. The game, which has been described as "polite baseball," is the most popular sport in India.

The Indian national cricket team is one of the best in the world. Its top players are treated like movie stars. Youngsters learn to play cricket on any empty ground. If they do not have real equipment, they use a piece of wood as a bat and anything round as a ball.

Cricket is a popular spectator sport, too, particularly games against India's neighbor, Pakistan. When the national team plays, people are glued to their TV sets.

Other popular sports in India include soccer; tennis; polo, which is played on horseback; and field hockey. The Indian men's field hockey team has won Olympic gold on eight occasions.

Contradictions in Education

India has the highest proportion of people who cannot read or write in the world. About 40 percent of Indians are illiterate. While most Indians agree that education is important, it is also expensive. School is only free up to age 11. After that, parents have to pay for books, tuition, and clothes: most students wear a school uniform.

Many children drop out of school to help earn income for their families.

University education is expensive. Only children from quite wealthy families can afford to go. They often study subjects that will help them get a good job, such as medicine, law, or information technology (IT). Ten years ago, an IT graduate from India had to move to find a good job, often to California. Today, they only have to go as far as Bangalore. The city has become one of the world's main computer centers.

▲ Some Indian schools are as good as any in the world—here girls study chemistry—but half of Indian children leave school by age 14.

Many Religions

India is a very spiritual country. It has no official religion, but is dominated by Hinduism. More than 80 percent of Indians are Hindu. The second most popular religion is Islam. Only 13 percent of Indians are Muslim—but that still means that India has one of the world's biggest Muslim populations. Other religions include Buddhism, Sikhism, and Jainism, which all began in India, and

COMPUTER WHIZ KIDS

Many children in India cannot read or write—but that doesn't mean that they're not smart. In 2001, Indian researchers set up a computer in a wall in a Delhi slum. They switched it on and left it. Children from the slum soon came to investigate. They started to play on the computer and click the mouse. Even though they could not read or understand English, it took them an average of only eight minutes before they were surfing the Net. After two months of trying out the computer, they were downloading and playing songs. The government hopes that the project might lead to a program that will help the country's poorest children use computers to learn to read and write.

Christianity. At the same time, many people from the West have become interested in Indian beliefs.

Most Hindu homes have some kind of shrine to one of the hundreds of gods. People in Mumbai traditionally revere Lakshmi, the goddess of wealth. Many homes have a statue of her, garlanded with flowers. Ganesha, the elephant god, and Hanuman, the monkey god, are favorites everywhere. Many *saddhus*, Hindu holy men, live with gray langur monkeys, which are also named Hanuman langurs for the god.

▲ Ganesha is one of the best-loved of the Hindu gods. People believe that he removes obstacles and will grant them success and prosperity if they pray to him.

Tandoor or Thali

Indian food is popular around the world. In the north, people eat meat, vegetables, and breads such as *naan* and *chapati*. These are cooked in clay ovens called *tandoors*. In the south, where many people are vegetarians, the main dish served is *thali*. That is a complete meal of vegetables, rice, Indian bread, and dessert all served in small containers on a single large plate. On the east coast, fish is the main food.

Almost everyone eats rice, bread, and *dhal*. Dhal is made from lentils and spices, and there are hundreds of different types. You could eat dhal every day for a year and never taste the same one twice!

Indian fast food is very different from burgers and fries. Snacks such as *bhelpuri* are sold in the street or on the beach. Bhelpuri is a tasty mixture of crispy noodles, puffed rice, potatoes, onion, coriander leaves, and a spicy chutney.

Coconut sellers are common beside Indian roads. They cut open fresh coconuts, and customers drink the milk inside through a straw. When they have finished, the coconut seller scrapes out the soft flesh for their customers to eat.

Sitars and Tablas

Indians love music. Taxi drivers play their cassette players as loud as they can, and radios blast out from stores. You often hear the sitar, an instrument that looks like a cross between a guitar and a violin—but does not sound like either. The sitar is traditionally accompanied by small hand drums known as *tabla*.

Every village has its own music and dances. There are dances for weddings, births, moving to a new home, and harvest time. Religious festivals also often involve dancing.

AT YOUR SERVICE

An industry has grown up to deliver lunch to workers in India's cities. At midday, crowds of *dhaba wallahs* wait at railroad stations around the cities. They are waiting for housewives to deliver their husbands' tiffin boxes. These tin containers hold lunches of rice, vegetables, and dhal. They keep the food hot while the dhaba wallahs travel into the city and deliver the tiffin boxes to offices. Although the dhaba wallahs may not read, they use a simple color-coded system. Virtually every single box gets delivered to the right address. After lunch, the dhaba wallahs collect the boxes and take them back to the stations.

▲ A dhaba wallah wheels a bike loaded with tiffin boxes through the streets of Delhi.

A
Booming
Economy

YOUNG GIRLS WALK BACK from the village well with as much water as they can carry. On their heads, they carry large metal pots full of water. Some have another pot tucked under an arm. These are just some of the millions of children across India who do chores to help their families. India has the world's largest number of workers under the age of 14. Although laws ban children from working in dangerous places like mines, or in hotels and restaurants, many employers take no notice. Often, families encourage children to take jobs such as knotting carpets or making fireworks. The extra income is really useful. And many children would rather work than go to school, especially when classrooms are crowded, so it is hard to learn.

◀ Fetching and carrying water is women's work in India. In dry areas, even young girls may spend up to six hours a day bringing water from distant sources to their homes.

POWER AND THE PEOPLE

India is divided into 28 states and seven union territories (see political map on the opposite page). Each state has its own government, with a governor and chief minister. Union territories are ruled directly by the national government based in Delhi.

India inherited its parliamentary government from the British. Another legacy of British rule is officials' love of forms and other paperwork. The administrative service has grown greatly since independence—but so has the number of regulations. Whenever they deal with the government, people have to stand in line for hours to get the right papers stamped and approved.

Trading Partners

India imports more goods than it exports. Its major exports include textiles, chemicals, leather, equipment used in engineering, gems, and jewelry. It imports oil, machinery, gems, and fertilizer. The European Union (27 countries) as a bloc is India's most important trading partner.

Country	Percent India exports
United States	16.7%
United Arab Emirates	8.5%
China	6.6%
All others combined	68.2%

Country	Percent India imports
China	7.3%
United States	5.6%
Switzerland	4.7%
All others combined	82.4%

► The Lok Sabha, or People's Assembly, in session in Delhi

KYRGYZSTAN

TAJIKISTAN

38°N

Boundary
claimed
by India

FLOATING
MARKET STALLS,
page 57

Boundary
claimed
by Pakistan

AFGHANISTAN

Boundary
claimed
by India

34°N

Boundary
claimed
by India

● Srinagar
JAMMU AND
KASHMIR

Boundary
claimed
by China

CHINA

MAP KEY

✪ National capital

◉ State or territory capital

0   miles   250

0   km   250

BOLLYWOOD
FILM SET,
page 56

HIMACHAL
PRADESH
◉ Simla

30°N

Boundary claimed
by China

PAKISTAN

PUNJAB
Chandigarh ◉

● Dehra Dun
UTTARAKHAND

BRICKWORKS,
page 53

HARYANA

ARUNACHAL PRADESH

PEOPLE'S
ASSEMBLY,
page 50

✪ New Delhi

NEPAL

SIKKIM
Gangtok ◉

BHUTAN

◉ Itanagar

Jaipur ●

UTTAR
PRADESH

DISPUR
◉

ASSAM

NAGALAND
● Kohima

GIRLS
CARRYING
WATER,
pages 3, 48-49

RAJASTHAN

● Lucknow

Shillong
MEGHALAYA

● Imphal
MANIPUR

26°N

◉ Patna
BIHAR

BANGLADESH

TROPIC OF CANCER

Agartala
◉
TRIPURA

● Aizawl

Gandhinagar ◉

JHARKHAND

WEST
BENGAL

MIZORAM

22°N

GUJARAT

Bhopal ●

MADHYA
PRADESH

Ranchi ●

Kolkata
(Calcutta)

MYANMAR
(BURMA)

Arabian Sea

DAMAN AND DIU

DADRA AND
NAGAR HAVELI

Raipur ●

CHHATTISGARH

ORISSA

● Bhubaneshwar

Bay of
Bengal

Mumbai ◉
(Bombay)

MAHARASHTRA

18°N

COTTON SPOOLS,
page 55

● Hyderabad

PUDUCHERRY

Panaji ◉
GOA

ANDHRA
PRADESH

14°N

KARNATAKA

Port Blair ●

PUDUCHERRY

Bangalore ◉

● Chennai
(Madras)

Kavaratti ●

◉ Puducherry (Pondicherry)

PUDUCHERRY

ANDAMAN AND
NICOBAR ISLANDS

10°N

KERALA

TAMIL
NADU

LAKSHADWEEP

Indian
Ocean

Thiruvananthapuram ◉
(Trivandrum)

SRI
LANKA

6°N

MALDIVES

Political Map

One Party, One Family?

After India gained independence from Great Britain in 1947, one political party—and just one family dominated politics. The Congress Party was led by Mahatma Gandhi's successor, Jawaharlal Nehru. Two years after Nehru's death in 1964, his daughter, Indira Gandhi, became prime minister. She was not related to Mahatma Gandhi, but sharing the same name helped her political career. She was prime minister for 15 years, with one brief gap. Her first son, Rajiv Gandhi, was prime minster for five years from 1984 to 1989.

The Gandhis had many enemies. Both Indira and

HOW THE GOVERNMENT WORKS

The federal government has two houses of parliament, the People's Assembly (Lok Sabha) and the Council of States (Rajya Sabha). Two members of the People's Assembly, the lower house, are appointed by the president; the rest are elected every five years. The president also chooses 12 members of the Council of States, the upper house. The remainder are elected for six-year terms. The president is chosen by the two houses and the members of the state parliaments. The president's role is ceremonial. It is the prime minister who has the real political power. He or she is the leader of the largest party in the People's Assembly. The prime minister heads the Council of Ministers, which is in charge of running the country. The justices of the Supreme Court are appointed by the president on the advice of the prime minister.

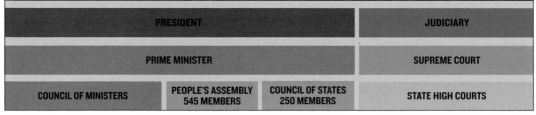

FEDERAL GOVERNMENT				
PRESIDENT			JUDICIARY	
PRIME MINISTER			SUPREME COURT	
COUNCIL OF MINISTERS	PEOPLE'S ASSEMBLY 545 MEMBERS	COUNCIL OF STATES 250 MEMBERS	STATE HIGH COURTS	

Rajiv Gandhi were killed. Indira Gandhi was killed by her own bodyguards. They were Sikhs who were angry because she had ordered an army attack on the Golden Temple at Amritsar, the Sikhs' holiest shrine. Rajiv

Gandhi was killed by Sri Lankan terrorists. They did not want India to be involved in a civil war in Sri Lanka.

With the death of Rajiv Gandhi, the Gandhi family disappeared from public view until 2004, when Rajiv Gandhi's Italian-born widow, Sonia, led the Congress Party in elections. Although the party won and she could have become prime minister, she chose not to take up the post.

▲ Portraits of India's former leaders—Mahatma Gandhi, Indira Gandhi, and Jawaharlal Nehru—appear with religious posters at this sidewalk stall.

▼ Women load bricks onto wheelbarrows. India is the world's second largest brick producer, but the work is hard and poorly paid.

Opposition Parties

A number of opposition parties have challenged the Congress Party's domination of Indian politics. None were successful until the rise of the Bharatiya Janata Party (BJP). The BJP is a Hindu nationalist party. It became very popular in the 1990s, when religious tensions between the majority Hindus and the minority Muslims flared up. During the last part of the

INDUSTRY & MINING

This map shows the location of India's chief mining operations and industrial centers. Iron ore, manganese, and chromite are mined in many places. The most abundant coal deposits are on the Chota Nagpur Plateau in eastern India. India's oldest industry is steel manufacturing, but the electronics industry is increasingly important.

MAP KEY

⚙ Manufacturing center

🏭 Steel manufacturing

🏭 Processing plant

⛏ Coal mining

Major Mines

Al Aluminum

Fe Iron ore

0 mi 400
0 km 400

HIMALAYA

Amritsar
Delhi
Kanpur
Ahmadabad
Al
Fe Jamshedpur
Nagpur
Mumbai (Bombay)
Hyderabad
Al
Asansol
Al
Kolkata (Calcutta)
Steel
Al Al
Bangalore
Fe
Chennai (Madras)
Cu
Indian Ocean

1990s, the BJP led a government that was made up of several other parties. In 2004 they suffered a surprise defeat. The Congress Party once again came to govern India.

Indian Giant

At the start of the 21st century, India's economy was a spectacular success story. It has grown so fast that experts predict it will soon become one of the world's leading economies, together with China.

Indians have always had a reputation for working hard. That goes from the man who mends shoes on the street to an executive in one of India's giant companies. Hard work is at the heart of India's boom, but there is another reason. Although many Indians are poorly educated, there are millions who are highly trained English-speaking college graduates. Indian scientists and engineers are particularly valuable to the economy. More and more Indians can afford to buy luxury items like jewelry, washing machines, and televisions. Indian factories must work harder to meet the demand. Between 2005 and 2006, for example, the number of Indians who used cell phones more than doubled, from 52 million to 123 million.

MAY I HELP YOU?

In a poll by American online company e-Loan, almost 85 percent of customers were happy to speak to an agent in India if it speeded up their loan application. Like other Western firms, e-Loan uses agents in India because they are less expensive and better educated than similar workers at home.

Salaries in India are about one-fifth of those in the United States. But the Indians who work in call centers are college graduates who speak fluent English and often other languages, too, and can solve any problems that come up. They enjoy a high standard of living compared to many Indians.

Silicon Valley, Indian Style

Bangalore is India's fastest-growing city. It is like California's Silicon Valley, the major IT center in the United States. Smart young people move to Bangalore to get jobs creating new computer software. The software industry in India has grown by 50 percent a year for the last few years. The money flowing into Bangalore has transformed the city in the last 20 years. There are restaurants, hotels, movie theaters, and shopping malls for the well-paid young workers. Real-estate prices are soaring, and rush-hour traffic backs up for miles.

▼ A young worker spins cotton thread onto hundreds of spools in a Mumbai textile factory.

BOLLYWOOD

India makes more movies than any other country. It also has one of the biggest audiences in the world—and one of the most critical. Mumbai is the home of the movie industry. It is popularly known as Bollywood, after Hollywood. Chennai (Madras) also has a thriving industry making movies in the languages of southern India.

Bollywood movies follow a set pattern: there is singing and dancing, a romance, lots of action and secret plans, and dramatic changes of luck. They always have a happy ending. Movies are usually about three hours long, with one intermission.

▲ Bollywood films generally contain songs and dances. The performers are huge stars, earning large fees, and are mobbed wherever they go. Their lives are reported in popular gossip magazines.

Farmers Left Behind

Mahatma Gandhi believed that India's heart lay in its villages, but today the countryside is missing out on India's boom. Since independence, farming has been a success story. More land was planted with crops, and new farming techniques were introduced to water the fields and control pests. The result became known as the "Green Revolution": India grew enough food to feed its own population for the first time. It no longer needed to import grain, for example.

But the advances in technology have mostly benefited large landowners. Most farms cover less than 3 acres (1.5 ha). Farmers grow just enough to feed their own families. They have nothing extra to sell, and no spare money to buy seeds or fertilizer. If they borrow money, they must repay the loan with a percentage of the crop. If a harvest fails because of poor rainfall, the farmers face large debts.

Looking Ahead

India has reasons to be confident. Its economy is still growing rapidly. Many people are enjoying a higher standard of living. In politics, the country is more stable than it has been for a long time. Talks have even begun with Pakistan about the disputed border in the state of Kashmir. But India also faces many challenges. It has the second highest population in the world, after China. So many people place great pressure on the environment. Much of the rural population lives in poverty. Indians look forward to becoming truly prosperous—when all of their people can enjoy a taste of their country's new wealth.

▲ Farmers jostle for position at Srinagar's floating vegetable market on Dal Lake.

Add a Little Extra to Your Country Report!

I f you are assigned to write a report about India, you'll want to include basic information about the country, of course. The Fast Facts chart on page 8 will give you a good start. The rest of the book will give you the details you need to create a full and up-to-date paper or PowerPoint presentation. But what can you do to make your report more fun than anyone else's? If you use your imagination and dig a bit deeper into some of the topics introduced in this book, you're sure to come up with information that will make your report unique!

>Flag

Perhaps you could explain the history of India's flag, and the meanings of its colors and symbol. Go to **www.crwflags.com/fotw/flags** for more information.

>National Anthem

How about downloading India's national anthem and playing it for your class? At **www.nationalanthems.info** you'll find what you need, including the words to the anthem, plus sheet music. Simply pick "I" and then "India" from the list on the left-hand side of the screen, and you're on your way.

>Time Difference

If you want to understand the time difference between India and where you are, this Web site can help: **www.worldtimeserver.com**. Just pick "India" from the list on the left. If you called India right now, would you wake whomever you are calling from their sleep?

>Currency

Another Web site will convert your money into rupees, the currency used in India. You'll want to know how much money to bring if you're ever lucky enough to travel to India: **www.xe.com/ucc**.

>Weather

Why not check the current weather in India? It's easy—simply go to **www.weather.com** to find out if it's sunny or cloudy, warm or cold in India right this minute! Pick "World" from the headings at the top of the page. Then search for India. Click on any city you like. Be sure to click on the tabs below the weather report for Sunrise/Sunset information, Weather Watch, and Business Travel Outlook, too. Scroll down the page for the 36-hour Forecast and a satellite weather map. Compare your weather to the weather in the Indian city you chose. Is this a good season, weather-wise, for a person to travel to India?

>Miscellaneous

Still want more information? Simply go to National Geographic's One-Stop Research site at **http://www.nationalgeographic.com/onestop**. It will help you find maps, photos and art, articles and information, games, and features that you can use to jazz up your report.

Glossary

Astronomer a scientist who studies the stars, planets, and other heavenly bodies.

Bonfire a large fire lit during celebrations.

Colony a region that is ruled by a nation located somewhere else in the world. Settlers from that distant country take the land from the region's original inhabitants.

Culture a collection of beliefs, traditions, and styles that belongs to people living in a certain part of the world.

Deposit a supply of a natural resource buried underground.

Destiny the main moments or final results of a person's life. Some people believe that their destiny is already decided and they are unable to change or avoid it.

Ecosystem a community of living things and the environment they interact with; an ecosystem includes plants, animals, soil, water, and air.

Financial relating to finance, the management of money by companies, governments, and individuals.

Hindu a follower of Hinduism, a religion founded in India that involves the worship of many different gods and spirits.

Illiterate unable to read.

Jain a follower of Jainism, a religion with similarities to Hinduism and Buddhism. Jains believe that they must not injure any other living thing. They even cover their mouths when walking to prevent breathing in flying insects by accident.

Monsoon a wind that changes direction twice a year. When the monsoon wind blows from the ocean, it brings a period of heavy rains. The regular rainy season is also often simply called "the monsoon."

Nationalism a belief or political movement that celebrates a certain nation or country. Nationalists believe that their government should not be controlled by another country.

Nonviolent protest a form of political protest developed by Gandhi in which people simply refuse to obey harsh or unfair laws.

Parallel to run alongside and never get closer or move farther apart.

Peninsula a narrow piece of land that is surrounded by water on three sides.

Sikh a follower of Sikhism, a religion founded in the Punjab by Guru Nanak. Sikh men always carry a dagger and never cut their hair or beard. The hair is covered by a turban.

Silt very fine soil and clay that is carried by large rivers. As it settles to the riverbed, silt forms deep mud.

Slum a district of a city where the poorest communities live in badly built homes without the water, power, and sewage services of more wealthy areas.

Species a type of organism; animals or plants in the same species look similar and can only breed successfully among themselves.

Tiffin a British term for a light lunch or picnic. Lunch boxes are known as tiffin boxes in India.

Union an agreement between regions or countries to join together as a single state.

Wallah the Indian word for a worker associated with a certain job or product. A dhobi wallah collects dirty laundry; a dhaba wallah carries boxes of food.

Bibliography

Brownlie Bojang, Ali. *Focus on India.* Milwaukee, WI: World Almanac Library, 2007.

Draper, Allison Stark. *India: A Primary Source Cultural Guide.* New York: PowerPlus Books, 2003.

Harkrader, Lisa. *India.* Berkeley Heights, NJ: MyReportLinks.com Book, 2004.

http://www.incredibleindia.org/ (travel guides, history, and cultural information)

http://india.gov.in/ (government Web site)

http://pmindia.nic.in/ (Indian prime minister's Web site)

Further Information

NATIONAL GEOGRAPHIC Articles

Toll, Roger. "India on High." NATIONAL GEOGRAPHIC ADVENTURE (February 2007): 18–20, 22.

Ward, Geoffrey C. "India: Fifty Years of Independence." NATIONAL GEOGRAPHIC (May 1997): 2–57.

Web sites to explore

More fast facts about India, from the CIA (Central Intelligence Agency): https://www.cia.gov/cia/publications/factbook/geos/in.html

India makes more movies each year than any other country. Take a look at the latest trailers from Bollywood, the largest movie industry in the world: http://www.bollywoodworld.com/trailers/

Want to know more about Hinduism? Take a look at this animated version of one of the religion's main stories: http://www.hindukids.org/ramayana/index.html

Take a virtual tour of the Taj Mahal, one of the world's most famous buildings: http://www.taj-mahal.net/augEng/main_screen.htm

Learn more about Mahatma Gandhi, the Indian leader who inspired civil-rights movements around the world: http://www.gandhiinstitute.org/

See, hear

There are many ways to get a taste of life in India, such as movies, CDs, magazines, or TV shows. You might be able to locate these:

Gandhi (1982)
A movie of the epic story of the life of the leader of India's independence movement.

Mahabharata
This is one of the main stories in Hinduism. It tells of the conflict between two families of superbeings. Most English translations are easy to read, and it's a good story, too.

Ravi Shankar
Even though he is in his 80s, Ravi Shankar is one of the best sitar players in the world. He began his career in the 1930s, but became world famous in the 1960s when he taught the Beatles about Indian music.

Times of India
You can find the main English-language Indian newspaper at: http://timesofindia.com. Check out the cartoons of Ninan's World for a lighter look at life in India.

Index

Credits

Picture Credits

Front Cover – Spine: Kharidehal Abhirama Ashwin/Shutterstock; Top: Justin Guariglia/NGIC; Low far left: Steve McCurry/NGIC; Low left: Michael Melford/NGIC; Low right: Michael Nichols/NGIC; Low far right: James P. Blair/NGIC.

Interior – Corbis: 14 up; Bob Krist: 17 up; Thom Lang: 59 up; NGIC: William Albert Allard: 45 up, 46 center, 53 lo, 56 up; James P. Blair: TP, 3 right, 30 lo, 44 up, 48-49; Richard Alexander Cooke III: 31 lo; Bruce Dale: 35 up; Jason Edwards: 23 lo, 33 lo; Bill Ellzey: 13 up; Marilyn Gibbons: 11 lo; Martin Gray: 31 up, 32 lo; Justin Guariglia: 2-3, 26-27, 34 lo; Catherine Karnow: 47 lo; Mattias Klum: 24 up; Frans Lanting: 20 lo,23 up; Steve McCurry: 2 left, 6-7, 16 lo, 36 up, 36 lo, 40 center, 42 lo, 50 lo, 53 up, 57 center; George F. Mobley: 25 up; Bobby Model: 10 up; Michael Nichols: 22 lo; Randy Olson: 28 up; Nicolas Reynard: 12 lo; Maria Stenzel: 43 lo; Pritt Vesilind: 37 lo; Cary Wolinsky: 3 left, 5 up, 38-39, 43 up, 55 lo; Michael S. Yamashita: 2 right, 15 up, 18-19, 25 lo.

Text copyright © 2007 National Geographic Society
Published by the National Geographic Society.
All rights reserved. Reproduction of the whole or any part of the contents without written permission from the National Geographic Society is strictly prohibited. For information about special discounts for bulk purchases, contact National Geographic Special Sales: ngspecsales@ngs.org

For more information, please call 1-800-NGS-LINE (647-5463) or write to the following address:

NATIONAL GEOGRAPHIC SOCIETY
1145 17th Street N.W.
Washington, D.C. 20036-4688 U.S.A.

Visit the Society's Web site at www.nationalgeographic.com

Library of Congress Cataloging-in-Publication Data available on request
ISBN: 978-1-4263-0127-8

Printed in the United States of America

Series design by Jim Hiscott.
The body text is set in Avenir; Knockout.
The display text is set in Matrix Script.

Front Cover—Top: Pilgrims visit the Taj Mahal; Low Far Left: View of Mumbai; Low Left: A musician with a sitar; Low Right: An Indian tigress and her cubs; Low Far Right: Sunrise at the Shore Temple, Mahabalipuram, Tamil Nadu State

Page 1—A boy learns to ride a bicycle at the village of Vadgam in Gujarat State; Icon image on spine, Contents page, and throughout: Henna-painted hands

Produced through the worldwide resources of the National Geographic Society

John M. Fahey, Jr., *President and Chief Executive Officer*; Gilbert M. Grosvenor, *Chairman of the Board*; Nina D. Hoffman, *Executive Vice President, President of Book Publishing Group*

National Geographic Staff for This Book

Nancy Laties Feresten, *Vice President, Editor-in-Chief of Children's Books*
Bea Jackson, *Director of Design and Illustration*
David M. Seager, *Art Director*
Virginia Koeth, *Project Editor*
Lori Epstein, *Illustrations Editor*
Stacy Gold, Nadia Hughes, *Illustrations Research Editors*
Priyanka Lamichhane, *Assistant Editor*
R. Gary Colbert, *Production Director*
Lewis R. Bassford, *Production Manager*
Maryclare Tracy, Nicole Elliott, *Manufacturing Managers*
Maps, *Mapping Specialists Ltd.*

Brown Reference Group plc. Staff for This Book

Volume Editor: Tom Jackson
Designer: Dave Allen
Picture Manager: Clare Newman
Maps: Encompass Graphics
Artwork: Darren Awuah
Index: Ann Barrett
Senior Managing Editor: Tim Cooke
Design Manager: Sarah Williams
Children's Publisher: Anne O'Daly
Editorial Director: Lindsey Lowe

About the Author

A. KAMALA DALAL is a British-born writer with an Indian father and an English mother. She has visited India countless times, both to stay with her family in Mumbai and to travel throughout the Subcontinent. Over the past thirty years she has witnessed India's remarkable economic transformation and says that the country is poised to become a major player on the world stage.

About the Consultants

PRADYUMNA P. KARAN is professor of geography at the University of Kentucky, United States. His research focuses on the environment and development in the Indian Subcontinent, Japan and Western China. He is the author of *The Non-Western World: Environment, Development and Human Rights* (Routledge, 2004) and *Japan in the 21st Century* (University Press of Kentucky, 2005).

DR. RAMESH CHANDRA DHUSSA, a native of India, (Dumka, Jharkhand) is a cultural geographer at Drake University, Des Moines, Iowa. He teaches the cultural, regional, and human geography of South Asia and India. In India he taught geography at the Magadh University, Bodh Gaya, Bihar. His research focuses on Literary and Humanistic geography, and various aspects of cultural, and ethnic geography of India. Professor Dhussa is a life member of the National Association of Geographers, India.